Ferrari 612 Scaglietti

by Julie Wilson

AXIS education

Acknowledgements

Cover design: Oliver Heath, Rafters Design

Photographs © Newspress and Ferrari

Copyright © Axis Education 2005

First published in Great Britain by Axis Education Ltd

ISBN 1-84618-015-5

Axis Education
PO Box 459
Shrewsbury
SY4 4WZ

Email: enquiries@axiseducation.co.uk

www.axiseducation.co.uk

If someone were to ask what you think the most glamorous job in the world is, what would you say? Super model? Premiership footballer? Celebrity hair stylist? You'd be wrong on all three counts, of course, for there is no more glamorous job than that of Ferrari test driver. Few people ever get the chance to sit in a Ferrari, let alone try them out for a living!

Just the name, Ferrari, makes you think of the high life, speed, wealth, St Tropez and beautiful people. Perhaps, when you daydream about what to do with your lottery winnings, you can see a Ferrari going nicely with the yacht and Malibu beach house. Perhaps, if performance cars are your thing, you just dream about being in control of such a high quality car.

Ferraris are, for some, symbols of a life that's out of reach. For others, they stand for master craftsmanship and expert design. Just to have the chance to drive one would fulfil a lifetime's wish list for many.

The Ferrari 612 Scaglietti.

Enzo Ferrari began building performance cars in 1947 at Modena, Italy. In 1943, the factory moved to Maranello, the site where they are still made today. He had driven for and run the Alfa Romeo racing team and decided to start his own car manufacturing company in 1938. It became known as the 'prancing horse' due to the emblem showing a horse rearing up on its hind legs. The car manufacturer Fiat bought half of the company in 1969 and the remainder in 1988 when Enzo died.

Ferrari always believed that racing cars were the models for road car designs and this still shows in the mixture of performance and comfort that is typical of Ferrari cars. Even now, the racetrack is used as a testing ground for the technology and research that goes into each vehicle.

Nine years after starting at Modena, Ferrari introduced the 125S. It was a 12-cylinder racing car which won its first race in May 1947, the same month that it first competed.

A modern-day Ferrari racing car.

In those days, it was normal for the bodies to be built by a variety of Italian coachbuilders. These included Touring, Vignale, Ghia and Farina. The engines also varied, from 90bhp to 155bhp, and the wheelbases ranged from 2160mm to 2620mm.

Enzo Ferrari's main passion was always motor racing and up until the late 1950s you could hardly tell the difference between his road and race cars. This would be impossible today, with the safety rules and manufacturing costs that make road and race cars very different.

Ferrari has continued to produce both types of car with huge success. The name has been making a strong impact on the world of Formula One since 1950, the year it began – lately with the help of Michael Schumacher!

Other famous drivers for Ferrari have included Fangio, Mike Hawthorn, Niki Lauda, Rubens Barichello and Alain Prost. The team is now the oldest in the championship and holds nearly every Formula One record.

Ferrari is famous in the world of motor racing.

All Ferraris were racing cars until 1948 when the first road car came out. This was the 166 Sport (later joined by the 166 Inter and 166 Mille Miglia). Ninety-two type 166 cars were built up until 1953.

The next road car was the 195. Twenty-five of these were made in 1951 until it was replaced by the 212, of which 80 were made until 1953. With so few made each time you begin to understand how Ferraris quickly gained a reputation for being exclusive, as well as being the top accessory for the rich. Enzo himself, however, was not pleased to have customers who were more worried about how the car made them look than how well it performed.

Ferrari's practice of using a variety of designers and coachbuilders changed in 1960 when Pininfarina became the standard designer and Scaglietti the standard coachbuilder. What has followed is a stream of high performance cars, with the first mid-engined car and the introduction of rear suspension in the 1960s. This is a design that has continued until recently.

The 612 Scaglietti is one of the latest in a long line of Ferrari performance cars.

Developed in 2001, the 612 was brought out as a successor to the 456M GTA, another 2+2 (two in the back, two in the front). It's a typical Ferrari four-seater grand tourer, yet it has been built with less than typical Ferrari technology.

By the 1980s Ferrari was making only mid-engined cars but when Fiat took over, the front mounted V12 engine was brought in again. The Ferrari 612 Scaglietti is different again, with a 'first for Ferrari' under the bonnet – all to do with the position of the engine.

The designers have come up with a layout that gives the best weight distribution by placing the engine behind the front axle. As a result, the centre of gravity is as far back and low as possible. This gives the 612 Scaglietti grand tourer the same kind of traction, cornering and braking ability as a Ferrari sports car.

The engine position is a 'first for Ferrari'.

The 612 Scaglietti is truly a thing of beauty. Its look was created by Pininfarina but its name is in honour of Sergio Scaglietti, an expert in the use of aluminium and believed by many to have created some of the most beautiful Ferrari bodies of the 1950s and 1960s.

True enough, its design carries the spirit and looks of Ferrari as well as the passion Ferrari has always shown for performance, technology and drama.

Known for styling its cars to resemble a curvy, female body, Ferrari has continued this tradition with the 612. On first view, you are struck by the unique 'Pininfarina' scalloped sides. These and the scooped lines running its length hark back to the heady days of 1950s Italy, when fashion and culture found a place in everything from travel to lifestyle.

The shape of the 612 Scaglietti carries the spirit and looks of Ferrari.

Ask anyone what a Ferrari is and they will tell you it's a fast, expensive, ultimate sports car, even if they have absolutely no interest in motoring. Such respect for a brand is summed up in one word: prestige – and it certainly isn't an interest in cars that makes you stand and stare at this one. The alloy wheels (18 inches at the front and 19 inches at the rear) are fitted with a stunning starfish design, making the 612 even more spellbinding to look at from the side.

There are special features, like the projector headlights that have see-through covers showing the inner workings. There are classic features, such as the high round tail lights that make the rear section look big and solid. Altogether, the curve of the wheel arches, the bonnet, cabin and tail give it an animal grace, like the thoroughbred, prancing horse of the company emblem.

This is the magic with Ferraris and the 612 Scaglietti is no exception. They are some of the most beautiful, sexy sports cars on the planet.

A special feature of the 612 Scaglietti is the projector headlights.

One of the most beautiful, sexy sports cars on the planet.

The 612 Scaglietti is the very first Ferrari 12-cylinder to have both the space frame chassis and body built from aluminium. This is the result of cutting edge production and assembly methods. The benefits of making them this way include a 60% increase in rigidity and a weight saving of 60kg compared to the 456M GTA, even though the 612 is actually larger.

The traditional Ferrari grille is in place, merging seamlessly with the headlamps and bodywork. The tail lamps sit snugly within the curvy rear haunches and are highlighted by their by soft, rippling ridges.

Just like the expert techniques used by Scaglietti years before, they mount the aluminium body panels on top of the structure and then weld and rivet them together. The use of aluminium as the main material for the chassis and body provides weight reduction, great handling and passenger safety all in one.

Ferrari uses the techniques of the coachbuilder Scaglietti when building the 612.

Curvy and sleek, female in character, Ferraris have been the obvious choice for many film directors, television directors, commercials and music video makers. They have appeared in 'Goldeneye', 'Dirty Rotten Scoundrels' and 'Rain Man' to name just three blockbuster movies. Madonna used one in her 'Material Girl' video and anyone old enough to remember 'The Persuaders' on TV in the 1970s will be able to picture Danny Wilde's Ferrari Dino 246.

It's no surprise, then, that getting into this car and cruising down the motorway feels like having a date with your favourite movie star. It draws the same kind of attention, for sure. People try to see if they can recognise the driver and other drivers chase you to get a longer look. For sheer beauty it's up there with the Aston Martin Vanquish – made famous by James Bond. Equally sexy, it's only a matter of time before the 612 Scaglietti joins its forerunners on the big screen.

The prancing horse – Ferrari's emblem.

The 612 Scaglietti has a fabulous, classy interior. The pressed or solid aluminium used to trim the inside is smart and decorative, giving it a mix of traditional style and modern soul. Life inside is made very pleasant by armrests carved out for rear passengers and hand-stitched leather in different shades on all trim materials. Sitting in the plush leather seats makes you feel the touch of luxury you'd expect from a Ferrari.

You also feel like you're sitting in a sporty, exclusive cabin with all the extra frills that include a dual-zone climate control system, a sound system made especially by Bose, a dusk sensor that automatically turns on the lights, a rain sensor that gets the windscreen wipers going, and an antitheft system.

At your feet, punched aluminium alloy pedals are joined by a similar passenger foot rest, highlighting the 612's loyalty to style – it isn't just the things you can see that have been given the aluminium treatment.

The classy interior of the 612 Scaglietti.

In fact, the inside is a haven of roomy, luxury chic.

Ferraris aren't generally known for having much space in the back. The term '2+2' usually means two seats up front with a small space behind them, also called 'seats' but only big enough to take a couple of friends for a short spin. There should be just enough time to let them see what you've got before the deep vein thrombosis sets in alongside the howls of pain.

This, however, is a genuine four-seater car. There is a real feeling of space and air inside – another 'first' for a Ferrari grand tourer – and 139mm more legroom than the 456M. The luggage compartment is a revelation, taking a six-piece luggage set without difficulty. With such a surprising amount of space for passengers and their bags, the 612 can easily cope with four occupants in comfort and still promise the excitement of a thrilling, sporty ride.

This isn't just a great-looking, high performance car from the most famous car manufacturer in the world. It's a family Ferrari.

The plush leather seats give that touch of luxury you'd expect from a Ferrari.

This Ferrari grand tourer has enough space to show your passengers what they're missing.

The inside is a haven of roomy, luxury chic.

The 612 has a low but comfortable driving position from its supple, leather bucket seats. The high-mounted, adjustable steering wheel has paddles to change gear with. The controls are at your fingertips.

With a big rev counter and speedometer that are easy to read, driving the 612 Scaglietti is a breeze. It's comfortable and pleasant in any conditions and it's safe. The aluminium construction makes it much more rigid and the braking and handling are high quality. This all means there is a higher level of safety for passengers in the event of a crash. In fact, this car exceeds international safety standards by a long way. Sensors in the engine that can recognise a sudden slowing down and alert the airbag system help, too!

The aluminium construction makes the 612 Scaglietti much more rigid than previous Ferraris.

On the road, though, it's something else.

Forget the right kind of sunglasses and six-figure income. Forget the St Tropez lifestyle and luxury yacht. Drive around in a Ferrari 612 Scaglietti like one of Enzo's ideal customers and be taken aback by the experience. Feel the thrill of handling this thoroughbred beauty, designed and built with a mix of tradition and new technology that keeps this car maker at the top of the performance car tree. Feel Ferrari history in your hands.

With a fuel tank that can cover 300 miles between stops, you really get the chance to see how equally happy the 612 Scaglietti is at low and high speeds. Hear the mellow burbling of the engine as you feel the performance go from gentle to fierce with no complaint from the car.

You can just keep going in a car with a fuel tank that covers 300 miles between stops.

Put your foot down and feel the car leap forward with enthusiasm. Suddenly you know why every boy's dream is to drive a Ferrari – it hugs the ground through twists and turns, turning with razor-like precision. With such a wide windscreen, you can place it in corners and bends with ease. You feel protected by the car's clever response to the brakes, as if it's concentrating as hard as you are.

With the 612, you get a choice of semi-automatic transmission or a manual six-speed gearbox. Either way, the clutch offers gear changes that are fast and smooth with no lurching around and no slipping.

This Ferrari takes bends with razor-like precision.

When you decide to take the plunge and really put your foot down, the acceleration is stunning. Your head snaps back and your body feels heavy with the force of 0 to 62mph (0 to 100kmh) in 4.2 seconds. In your ears, the engine screams gloriously – enjoying itself at high speed as much as you are.

It's a joy to realise you're in control. Where you go, and how fast, is up to you and nobody else.

Listen to the high-speed pleasure of the engine.

Ferrari 612 Scaglietti – king of the road.

The 612 presents the car-manufacturing world with a whole new set of car-making skills. It has been described as a 'dramatic new supercar' – a fair description of a car whose top speed is 196mph (315kmh). The classiness of its design and the levels of performance it can reach make it a perfect car. It's a car that carries the glamour of the 1950s and 1960s alongside modern-day ability. With a big boot, a big engine and a big design, the 612 is fast, practical and full of style.

The dramatic new supercar.

As thoroughbred as the horse on its grille.

With this car, Ferrari has pulled off an instant classic. It's a perfect mix of performance and comfort that can hold four people in high-speed luxury and safety.

An iconic machine, the 612 has passion, beauty and bravery. Its sexiness fills your vision. Shamelessly grand, it satisfies the customers that want elegance and control as well as blistering performance. Coming from a factory that makes only three to four thousand Ferraris per year, it also satisfies any longings to own an exclusive car.

The 612 Scaglietti is a fabulous car. It's a Ferrari.

Elegance, control and blistering performance. It's a Ferrari.

Technical specification – Ferrari 612 Scaglietti

Make	Ferrari
Model	612 Scaglietti
Engine size	5748cc
Top speed	199 mph (315km/h)
Acceleration	0–62 mph (0–100km/h) in 4.2 seconds
Fuel tank capacity	110 litres
Price	£170,500
Weight	1840kg
Transmission	6-speed manual or paddle-shift, rear-wheel drive
Wheelbase	2950mm
Tyres	245/45 ZR18 front, 285/40 ZR19 rear

Glossary

acceleration	how fast the car speeds up
accessory	something you have, or wear, that is extra to your clothes and makes you look good
alloy wheels	stylish wheels made of a blend of metals and bigger in size than standard wheels
aluminium	a lightweight metal, silver in colour
antitheft system	the car's security system, i.e. alarm and/or immobiliser
bhp	brake horse power (a measure of the power needed to stop a moving vehicle)
big rev counter	the dashboard dial showing the car's engine revolutions (how many times the engine turns over per second)
bucket seats	seats designed to 'hug' your bottom (and be more comfortable)
capacity	how much petrol the engine can hold
cc (cubic centimetres)	a measure of engine capacity
centre of gravity	the place at which weight comes to rest in any object or body.
coachbuilders	car body builders
convertible	a car whose roof can be put down
cylinders	metal tubes that work together to get the petrol to the engine. The more cylinders you have, the more powerful the car.
deep vein thrombosis	a dangerous condition where the blood stops flowing in the leg and a clot forms (usually caused by sitting for long periods with little room to stretch out)
dual-zone climate control system	control of temperature in front and rear of the car
forerunners	those that went before

grille	the framework on the front of the car lattice
handling	the way the car drives
iconic	like an icon, an idol, something or someone you look up to
manual 6-speed gearbox	a gear system you operate yourself
mid-engined	where the engine is placed in the middle area of the car
paddles	in a car, these are levers mounted onto the steering wheel for changing gear
projector headlights	headlights that lift up when turned on and fold away when turned off
punched aluminium pedals	pedals decorated with a 'honeycomb effect'
razor-like precision	perfect accuracy
scalloped	shaped like a curved shell
semi-automatic transmission	a type of gear system
chassis	the framework of the car
St Tropez	a resort in the South of France usually associated with the rich and famous
tail lights	the rear lights of a car
technical specification	information about the workings of the car
thoroughbred	pure-bred, pedigree
traction	grip on the road
transmission	another word for gearbox
wheelbase	the distance between the front and rear wheels